Pocket Guide to
CARNIVAL
GLASS

CW00644154

Schiffer Publishing Ltd

80 Lower Valley Road, Atglen, PA 19310 USA

Monica Lynn Clements

and Patricia Rosser Clements

Dedication

In memory of Eugene "Blue" Moon

Copyright © 2001 by Monica Lynn Clements and Patricia Rosser Clements
Library of Congress Card Number: 00-104151

Designed by "Sue"
Type set in UnivrstyRoman Bd BT/Humanst521 BT

ISBN: 0-7643-1197-2
Printed in China
1 2 3 4

Published by Schiffer Publishing Ltd.
4880 Lower Valley Road
Atglen, PA 19310
Phone: (610) 593-1777; Fax: (610) 593-2002
E-mail: Schifferbk@aol.com
Please visit our web site catalog at
www.schifferbooks.com or
write for a free catalog.

We are always looking for authors to write books on new and related subjects. If you have an idea for a book, please contact us at the above address.

This book may be purchased from the publisher.
Please include $3.95 for shipping.

In Europe, Schiffer books are distributed by
Bushwood Books
6 Marksbury Ave.
Kew Gardens
Surrey TW9 4JF England
Phone: 44 (0)208 392-8585;
Fax: 44 (0)208 392-9876
E-mail: Bushwd@aol.com
Free postage in the UK. Europe: Air mail at cost.
Please try your bookstore first.

Contents

Acknowledgements

Our gratitude goes to the many Carnival Glass collectors who shared their collections and their knowledge about this fascinating glass. We would also like to thank the following contributors whose beautiful glass appears in the following pages: Jerre Barkley, Karen Braswell, Pat Canfield, Ollie Clements, Virginia Giles, Pat Henry of Yesterday's Rose, Roland Hill, Mary Liles, Margaret McRaney of Jennie's Antique Mall, Mary Gene Moon, Kenneth L. Surratt, Jr., Marie Taylor, Barbara Vreeland of Garden Gate Antiques, Texarkana, Texas; Bill Williams of Gold Leaf Antique Mall, Jefferson, Texas; and Yesterday's Antiques Mall, Atlanta, Texas.

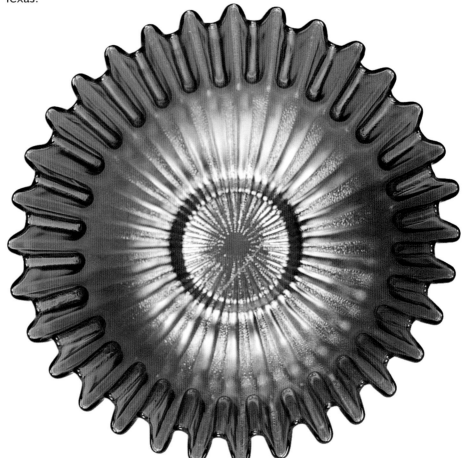

Introduction

The world of Carnival Glass is vast. With the large variety of patterns, the study of this area of glass is truly the study of history. Examining the shapes, colors, motifs, and the quality of iridescence tells us what people of a bygone era chose to use in their homes.

Another noteworthy category of Carnival Glass that deserves study is contemporary glass. With the revival of Carnival Glass that occurred in the 1960s, a number of patterns were reissued. A plethora of colorful pieces are on the market, many of them coming from old molds of companies no longer in business. This glass is less expensive but no less valued to collectors who favor this colorful and plentiful glass.

What we have done in this book is to give an overview of classic Carnival Glass. Prices of selected pieces in certain colors can be found along with the photographs. This book showcases nearly eighty patterns of classic Carnival Glass.

We have also included a chapter on contemporary glass that includes reissues of classic Imperial patterns as well as pieces from Indiana, Joe St. Clair, Fenton, and Westmoreland. While the list is not complete, this pocket guide does give a good variety of what collectors may find on their search for Carnival Glass.

As with any book of this nature, the prices are to be used as a guide only. We have attempted to be fair in the pricing, but we realize that prices will vary according to what part of the country you are in.

Chapter One
The Story of Carnival Glass

What Carnival Glass Is

The definition of Carnival Glass is a simple one—it is iridised glass. "Carnival Glass" could be considered a misnomer for iridised glass, as it conjures up memories of prizes given away at carnivals or fairs. However, iridised glass has a rich history that precedes the days in which wholesalers cleaned out their warehouses of surplus, choosing to sell what was once popular glass for prizes or souvenirs.

The process of producing the rich iridescence on glass began with glass made in molds or glass that was blown. The piece was taken out of the mold, and could be reheated and shaped in a number of ways. Then came the all-important step: the glass was sprayed with a chemical substance that produced an iridised lustre that gave the glass a colorful metallic sheen. Some pieces were sprayed only on the exterior with the iridescence, while other items, such as bowls, got the spraying treatment on both the inside and outside.

Another variation was glass that was shaped *after* it had been sprayed. This shaping created what collectors call stretch glass. One telltale characteristic of stretch glass is a surface with cracks that resembles onionskin. Several companies made stretch glass.

The Industrial Age had much to do with the origination of Carnival Glass. In an era of mass production and more efficient means of travel, manufacturers were able to create a kind of glass that was distinctive and could brighten up Victorian households. As an alternative to the expensive art glass of the day, Carnival Glass was affordable to everyone.

Motifs

With the amazing number of patterns in classic Carnival Glass, a valid question arises. How did manufacturers decide what motifs to use for their patterns? The answer is a simple one—companies chose what appealed to consumers.

Naturalistic subjects became commonplace. The result could be found through patterns depicting butterflies and birds. For example, several companies offered the Peacock at the Urn motif. Other variations on peacocks proved to be big sellers such as the Peacock at the Fountain pattern. An array of examples can be found showcasing butterflies. Birds also played an important role in motifs.

Animals were another naturalistic motif that endured for hundreds of years and experienced a resurgence during the Art Nouveau movement in the late 1800s. Victorians utilized the dramatic effect of animals in their décor. Patterns existed that featured such animals as elks, horses, lions, panthers, and the like. Fenton had the distinction of creating many of the popular animal patterns featured in the Carnival Glass of the day.

The Victorians were avid horticulture enthusiasts. Flowers were prevalent in artwork, books, handwork, and jewelry of the period. It came as no surprise that flowers found their way onto Carnival Glass. The popularity of Imperial's Lustre Rose is evidence of what consumers liked. Other companies created their own floral motifs.

Fruit depictions offered an alternative to the more traditional flowers. Each company created its own fruit patterns. Perhaps no fruit was so popular as the grape. Many companies created patterns featuring grapes. For example, Northwood, Fenton, and Imperial each had its own version of the Grape and Cable pattern.

Another category was a type of pattern known simply as "near-cut." The designs coming from "near-cut" pieces were geometric. These pieces filled the void for consumers who wanted to achieve the look of more expensive cut glass. Although many companies created their own patterns of "near-cut" glass, Imperial experienced great success with their offerings in this area with shapes that approximated the look of cut glass.

The craze for Carnival Glass endured until the 1930s when the glass fell out of favor with consumers. The surplus glass was sold wholesale and appeared at fairs and carnivals where it was offered as prizes. Carnival Glass holds great fascination for collectors and offers many hours of study for the glass enthusiast.

The Shapes

Glass companies produced a multitude of shapes in Carnival Glass. Starting out with vases and bowls, the choices quickly expanded. Such companies as Imperial had the reputation for producing glassware that was sturdy and functional. Thus, examples exist of breakfast sets, dressing table sets, punch bowls and cups, table sets, water sets, and the like. Other items for the table were candy and nut bowls. Fruit bowls and banana bowls in iridescent colors provided colorful accents on tables. The list of pieces is endless, and many examples of interesting shapes can be seen in the following pages.

Left. Fruit Lustre ("Fruits") tumbler by Federal Glass Company. $38-42.
Center. Peacock at the Fountain by Northwood tumbler. $56-90.
Right. Lustre Rose by Imperial tumbler. $21-23.

Along with being functional, vases held great decorative value. They came in different shapes and sizes, although the swung vase was prominent during the era of classic Carnival Glass. The process for creating this type of vase was just as the name implied. The maker took the vase from the mold while the glass was warm, and swung the vase to achieve the stretched effect. The sizes of these interesting and functional vases vary from 3" to a truly spectacular 22".

Other shapes of vases existed that were of the molded variety and were known as unswung vases. Other vases were blown. These kinds of vases have been sought after by collectors. An example is Imperial's Loganberry vase.

Another item that held flowers was the rosebowl. Instantly recognizable, the bowl had legs or a collar base and always had the turned-in top.

Left. Fine Rib vase by Fenton. $50-80.
Center. Fine Rib vase by Fenton. $42-68.
Right. Flute vase by Fenton. $40-52.

Loganberry vase by Imperial. $250-330.

The actual shape of a piece of glass depended upon the artisan. A variety of edges can be seen in Carnival Glass. Each company produced its own effects and embellishments. For example, Fenton utilized its distinctive ruffle while Northwood originated a pie crust edge on many of its pieces. The candy ribbon edge was common among makers. These different edges were made during the molding process when the glass was reheated and shaped by hand.

Green Nippon bowl with ruffled edge by Northwood.
$275-375.

Amethyst Stippled Rays bowl by Northwood, shown to highlight the candy ribbon edge.
$50-75.

The Basic Colors of Carnival Glass

The color of Carnival Glass does not refer to the iridised color, but to the color of the base glass. The base color can be determined by holding the glass to the light.

Amethyst

Often a difficult color to describe, Amethyst is similar to purple, although not as dark. A pale amethyst color resembles lavender, a color seen in some creations by Dugan, Imperial, Millersburg and Northwood.

Blue

A color of varying hues in Carnival Glass, blue can be found in a light color or an aqua teal. Many collectors favor the richness of cobalt blue. Imperial liked using cobalt blue. Northwood has been seen as a company that produced great amounts of Carnival Glass in blues while Dugan and Millersburg also utilized blues for their creations.

Clambroth

Clambroth is a color similar to marigold, but the color is clear. The iridescence provides clambroth with its ginger ale color.

Green

Green comes in a spectrum of colors, from the darker hues to lighter ones, with many shades in between. All major Carnival Glass manufacturers made some type of green iridised glass. The shade depended upon the company's whim. For example, Imperial created a shade known as Helios, that was a light shade of green with silvery iridescence. Other companies such as Northwood made dishes in an icy green. The possibilities were endless.

Marigold

Perhaps the signature color for Carnival Glass, marigold is abundant. It comes in many different hues, from light to dark. Going against the rule of the base color providing the color of the glass, marigold has a clear base color with marigold iridescence.

White

White Carnival Glass was created by iridising clear glass and then treating the glass in such a way that it looked frosted.

Opalescence

The process that turns edges of Carnival Glass a milky white color was perfected by several companies, although Dugan excelled at creating pieces of opalescent Carnival Glass. The formula for this process consisted of adding bone ash to the regular mixture in a batch. The glass was reheated, and the amount of reheating affected whether there would be opalescence over a large part of the piece or only around the edges. Once this process was completed, the glass was sprayed with iridescence. Often, marigold was the common color for opalescent pieces.

Wreathed Cherry bowl by Dugan in peach opalescent.

Decorated Ware

The process of enameled decoration on glass preceded the Carnival Glass craze. But by 1911, such companies as Dugan, Fenton, and Northwood offered Carnival Glass with enameled decoration. Fruit and flowers proved to be popular motifs. What makes these pieces interesting is that each artisan had his or her own style of adorning the piece.

Four rare cobalt blue tumblers from Spring Festival by Northwood. $65-75 each.

Major Producers of Carnival Glass

Dugan

What would soon become the Dugan Glass Company started out as the Indiana Glass Company. This operation began on April 14, 1892, in Indiana, Pennsylvania. Harry White was the president, but the company closed in less than a year.

Harry Northwood first leased the building and eventually bought it. His new venture began in 1895, and for the following two years, Northwood glass was produced there. This venture, known as Northwood Glass Company, was one in which Harry Northwood took as his partners his wife and his aunt and uncle, Thomas and Anne Dugan. The name of the plant was later changed to Dugan Glass Company, with Thomas Dugan as the overseer, along with W.G. Minnemeyer.

The glass produced here was made from Northwood molds. Then, in 1913, the name of the company changed to Diamond Glass Company. The plant continued to manufacture decorative and functional glassware, but the molds were changed so that the mark on the glassware became a "D" within the diamond design. Unfortunately, a fire destroyed the factory in 1931, and the effects of the Great Depression kept the factory from being rebuilt.

Fenton

Fenton Glass Company set the standards for many of the glass companies of the day who labored to produce Carnival Glass. Fenton has thrived and continues to produce fine art glass in the present day.

In 1906, Frank L. Fenton and his brother John decided to start their glass company in Martins Ferry, Ohio. A new location was decided upon, and 1907 found Williamstown, West Virginia, for the new site of the factory. This is where the current factory is located.

Frank Fenton displayed his affinity for marketing and a gift for design that captured the attention of the public. The company's iridised creations met with great success. When the Indiana Tumbler and Goblet Company went out of business, Frank Fenton brought in the talented Jacob Rosenthal, who proved a valuable asset to the company because of his understanding of how to adorn glass.

In 1907, the company began producing glass with a metallic lustre that was referred to as "Iride" or "Iridill" glass—what we now know as Carnival Glass. John Fenton departed the company to form Millersburg Glass Company in 1908, and by this time, the Carnival Glass bonanza had begun at the Fenton Glass Company. Fenton made its mark in Carnival Glass with its wide production that continued into the 1920s. For a time, the iridised glass was more popular than other lines that the company produced. Unlike many companies, Fenton managed to outlast the Depression years.

In 1970, the company began to reissue patterns of Carnival Glass. Today, it continues to create outstanding examples of iridised glass for collectors.

Like other companies, Fenton's Carnival Glass came in a variety of colors. They did, however, produce certain colors that were made only at the Fenton Glass Company. For example, during the 1920s, two distinctive colors were debuted, Red and Celeste Blue.

Imperial Glass Company

The story of the Imperial Glass Company began in 1901 when Edward Muhleman organized the venture for his glass company. The site chosen for the factory was in Bellaire, Ohio, and the production of glass began in 1904.

From the start, Imperial designed its glass for mass production. The lines of glassware soon appeared in F.W. Woolworth's stores. Imperial glass stood out from the rest because of its versatility. While other companies made decorator items, Imperial's goal was to produce glassware that could be used, and this glassware was heavier than that of other companies. Common items found coming from Imperial were milk pitchers, punch sets, stemware, table sets, vases, water sets, and the like.

Imperial entered the Carnival Glass market with enthusiasm. While Imperial began production of its extensive line of Carnival Glass, it wasn't until 1910 that the glass appeared in catalogs. During the era when Carnival Glass experienced the greatest popularity (from the early 1900s until 1930), Dugan, Fenton Art Glass Company, Millersburg, and Westmoreland introduced its own lines. No company was as prolific as Imperial, and no other company could match the quality of the iridescence. Another innovation was the introduction of stretch glass in 1910.

While Imperial offered patterns depicting naturalistic themes, it introduced distinctive "near-cut" pieces. The geometric patterns were popular, and consumers liked the look of the glass that mirrored the more expensive cut glass pieces available to consumers.

The company enjoyed success with its Carnival Glass lines, but the Great Depression brought an end to the days of mass production for many glass companies. Imperial was able to outlast the grim years of the Great Depression by changing to production of colored glass that we now know as Depression Glass. The company flourished after World War II until the 1960s.

With the advent of the 1960s came a renewal of interest in Carnival Glass at Imperial. The company used the old molds to reissue long-forgotten patterns. This revival played a pivotal role in ensuring the popularity of Carnival Glass for learned glass collectors and new collectors alike.

During the 1970s, the last chapter of the story of Imperial began. The company was sold to Lenox Inc., of New Jersey. The reissues of Carnival Glass continued under the company's new name—IGC Liquidating Corporation. The 1980s saw the company change hands several times until the doors of the company were closed in the late 1980s.

Imperial produced Carnival Glass in an array of colors. Like the other companies of the day, there was no shortage of marigold. Imperial created base colors that no other company could duplicate—Sapphire, Helios, a green shade with silver/gold iridised patina, and Clambroth, a shade similar to ginger ale or a light marigold. Among other colors that had success was Emerald, a brilliant green color. Imperial's purple color was a distinctive rich, deep hue that could not be copied. Cobalt blue is considered a rare color to find, as is the white. Red does exist but is prized by collectors because it is so hard to find.

A wide spectrum of colors appealed to glass enthusiasts with the reproduction of Carnival Glass in the 1960s. The colors that fared well in the past such as Rubigold (known as marigold), and Peacock (known as smoke), made a return. Amber, Amethyst, Aurora Jewels (known to collectors as cobalt), Azure Blue, an ice blue color, Helios Green, Pink, and Meadow Green (known as emerald), are just a few of the colors used for the reissued pieces.

Millersburg

John Fenton left Fenton Glass Company with the goal of starting his own company. For over a year, Fenton searched for the right place for his factory. He decided on Holmes County, Ohio, as the site for his company. He began the groundbreaking on September 14, 1908, and Millersburg Glass Company was in business.

John Fenton became the president of the company, and he named his brother, Robert Fenton, as Secretary of the company. Robert left in 1910 to rejoin Fenton Glass Company. On May 20, 1909, the production of glass began. The molds utilized had been designed by John Fenton. Several notable patterns emerged, including "Goddess of the Harvest," a design in honor of John Fenton's wife.

Fenton took pride in the excellent quality of the glass his factory produced. He offered free samples to visitors. People coming to the Millersburg factory could expect to receive a toothpick holder from the Ohio Star pattern. Fenton also arranged for his workers to receive gifts of plates made at the factory. While the gifts of Carnival Glass made many people happy, it didn't help the company thrive.

What distinguishes Millersburg glass from other glass, besides its quality, was the short lifespan of the company. While John Fenton was an ambitious man who wanted to do great things with his company, he didn't possess an affinity for making strong business decisions. The result was that Millersburg Glass Company became a debt-ridden operation, and the company claimed bankruptcy in 1911.

Since the Millersburg Glass Company was in operation for a short four years, there was not a huge variety of shapes available. While there were some plates and vases, perhaps what the company was most famous for was its bowls.

A color that set Millersburg Glass Company apart was its radium iridescence. Matt iridescence was another color produced by this company. The company relied on three main colors—Amethyst, Green, and Marigold. Today, collectors prize the few pieces in the colors of blue or vaseline that came from this company.

Northwood Glass Company

A dynamo of the glass industry, Harry Northwood started the Northwood Glass Company at the age of 27. The date his company went into operation was 1887, and the location was Martins Ferry, Ohio. The son of English glassmaker John Northwood, Harry Northwood merely joined the family business when he decided to go into glassmaking.

To prepare for the day when he'd have his own company, Harry Northwood took a job in 1880 with Hobbs, Brockunier and Company of Wheeling, West Virginia. After he had learned the trade, he moved to a position at La Belle Glass Company in Bridgeport, Ohio. It was here that he gained experience as a manager in 1887. Another job followed at the Buckeye Glass Company, located in Martin's Ferry, Ohio, where he stayed until 1896. At this time, he formed the Northwood Company and chose Indiana, Pennsylvania, for this endeavor.

Harry Northwood began a successful business, and he entered into the competitive glass trade. But he moved his company several times until he took the Hobbs Brockunier factory in Wheeling, West Virginia. It was here in 1902 that he allowed his genius to flourish.

When Fenton successfully introduced Carnival Glass in 1907, Harry Northwood utilized molds he'd used for earlier pressed glass. The result was the beginning of iridised glass at Northwood Glass Company. In 1908, the company debuted its marigold color, known as Golden Iris. Northwood's most popular pattern became Grape and Cable. The company had great success with its Carnival Glass with over 150 patterns; the manufacture of Carnival Glass continued until Harry Northwood's death in 1919. Without his innovative genius, the company's days were numbered, and Northwood Glass Company closed its doors in 1925.

Northwood's Carnival Glass came in a multitude of colors. Aqua Opal was an original color. The company favored the use of pastel colors such as ice blue, ice green, and white. Hues of blues and greens also proved popular choices such as Renninger Blue, Sapphire, and Teal. Unlike most companies, Northwood chose not to use red on their creations.

Later Carnival Glass

By the 1930s, Carnival Glass had gone out of style. A few companies continued to produce iridised glass although the level of production was no where near the output that came from the glory days of Carnival Glass.

From the years of the Great Depression until the 1950s, companies offered inexpensive pieces for their lines of what we now know as Depression Glass. Since manufacturers used inexpensive methods for making the glass, they used equally inexpensive methods for decorating the glass with iridescence. A common way of adorning the glass was by spraying on the iridescence, although the colors did not equal earlier Carnival Glass.

A variety of popular Depression Era patterns included iridescent pieces. For example, the Federal Glass Company offered an iridescent sheen on Bouquet and Lattice ("Normandie") and another pattern, Madrid. For Jeannette Glass

Company, the lines that received the iridescent treatment were Iris and Herringbone. The iridized pieces in this pattern appeared as reissues in 1969. In the 1940s, Jeannette introduced iridescent pieces in Anniversary and another pattern, Holiday ("Buttons and Bows"). In the 1950s, the company offered Louisa ("Floragold"), a reproduction of an earlier pattern by Westmoreland.

Bouquet and Lattice ("Normandie") bowl by Federal Glass Company. $19-35.

An alternate view of Bouquet and Lattice ("Normandie") bowl.

Louisa ("Floragold") candlestick by Jeannette Glass Company. $40-65.

Novelty Items

Since the early days of Carnival Glass, novelty items have been produced. These interesting pieces enjoyed great popularity during the 1920s and 1930s. What falls into this category can be anything from powder jars with figures on top to banks, and the list goes on. These mass produced items are still being made in the present day.

What is the purpose of these novelty items? A selected number of items have been used for company premiums although a large majority of novelties have found their way into gift shops. Numerous companies such as Anchor Hocking Glass Company, Imperial, Jeanette, and Joe St. Clair have produced novelty ware.

Three Joe St. Clair bells. $10-15 each.

Suzanne cobalt blue bell by
Imperial. $40-50.

Another view of bell to
highlight cobalt blue glass.

Hat-shaped toothpick holder by
Imperial. $45-55.

Footed green shell nappy by Westmoreland Glass Company. $20-45.

Another view of green shell nappy by Westmoreland Glass Company.

The Resurgence of Carnival Glass

A renewed interest in Carnival Glass began in the 1960s. **Imperial Glass Company** began to reissue its old patterns such as Lustre Rose and Windmill as well as several of the near-cut patterns. The reissued pieces bear the IG mark. The Imperial/Lenox pieces have the IGL mark. Another way to tell the reissued glass is by the feel of it. These pieces are thicker and heavier since they were made to be used.

While Imperial introduced important lines from the past, the Pastel Swan also made another appearance. Every company produced its own version of the Pastel Swan thirty years earlier. This item made a return in the 1960s and is now found in many different colors and often without a mark.

Green Pastel Swan salt. $150-175.

Pink Pastel Swan salt. $35-45.

Large swan. $85-95.

Large marigold swan. $90-100.

Glass enthusiasts are well acquainted with the **Deganhart** name. A wide variety of glass items from animals to paperweights came from Deganhart. The glass made by this company was iridised by other firms such as Joe St. Clair.

The **Hansen Brothers**, Richard and Robert, have made their mark iridising glass of other companies as well as creating their own art glass. The Hansens perfected their formula for iridization in the 1960s and began iridising glass made by a variety of companies. But the brothers began to create their own glass, much of it has a pontil mark. The brothers now work separately, and the pieces produced later have initials or their signatures. The art glass creations are much sought after and bring high prices.

Another company that enjoyed success with its iridised glass in the 1970s was **Indiana Glass Company** of Dunkirk, Indiana. While the company began in 1904, it wasn't until 1971 that it began to produce inexpensive Carnival Glass. The glass contained a sticker identifying the company. One of Indiana Glass Company's most notable offerings was the Harvest line.

Box for wedding bowl by Indiana Glass Company, ca. 1970s.

Pair of Lustre Rose reissued tumblers by Imperial. $15-20 each.

Smoke colored Lustre Rose reissued water set by Imperial. $175-195.

Lustre Rose reissued covered butter dish by Imperial. $20-30.

Pink Lustre Rose reissued covered butter dish by Imperial. $20-30.

Octagon smoke-colored
reissued compote by Imperial.
$15-25.

Joe St. Clair was a company that
iridised glass for other companies, but
Joe St. Clair also designed and iridised glass. The company is known primarily
for its novelty items.

Like Indiana Glass Company, the **L.E. Smith Glass Company** of Mount
Pleasant, Pennsylvania, began to produce Carnival Glass in the early 1970s. This
company began in 1905, and Depression glass enthusiasts are familiar with the
work of this company through its famous pattern, Mount Pleasant.

L.E. Smith's foray into Carnival Glass began with limited edition plates, one
depicting John F. Kennedy and another featuring Abraham Lincoln. The company moved into the direction of offering traditional styles of Carnival Glass in
such colors as amethyst, amber, green, and crystal lustre. The company continues to manufacture glass in the present day. The pieces made by L.E. Smith are
marked with an "S" sometimes found in a square or with the initials G and C.

Of course, these are just a few companies who have offered what is now
known as contemporary Carnival Glass. While there are those collectors who
think the more recent glass cannot rival the classic Carnival Glass, there are
those glass collectors who prize the newer creations. The reissued glass is often
easy to spot because of its color and the feel of the glass.

The fact that Carnival Glass is still treasured in its original as well as its more
contemporary forms is a testament to the men who toiled to create such beautiful glass during the classic iridescent glass years. This rich glass represents a
part of our history. This guide is an attempt to present a glimpse into that history
through the work of masterful craftsmen who created iridised glass.

Chapter Two
Carnival Glass Patterns

Acorn by Fenton

Bowl, ice cream, round, or ruffled, 7-9"		Blue	$45-75
Amberina	$485-725	Green	$110-195
Amethyst	$200-275	Marigold	$55-75
Aqua	$85-165	Red	$425-875

April Showers by Fenton

Vase, 7" and less	
Amethyst	$70-110
Blue	$55-78
Marigold	$55-85
Vase, 8"-15"	
Amethyst	$60-98
Blue	$60-98
Marigold	$35-45

Apple Blossoms by Dugan

Small Apple Blossoms marigold bowl. $20-30.

Butterfly & Berry by Fenton

Berry Set, with six or seven pieces		Creamer		
Amethyst	$420-645	Blue	$95-165
Marigold	$190-250	Marigold	$65-95
Bowl, large berry		Sugar, covered		
Amethyst	$150-225	Marigold	$70-110
Blue	$95-175		
Marigold	$65-100	Pitcher		
		Marigold	$175-325
Bowl, small berry			
Amethyst	$38-60	Tumbler		
Blue	$25-35	Blue	$45-75
Marigold	$25-35	Marigold	$20-30
Red	$650-950		
		Water set, 7 pieces		
Butter dish, covered		Blue	$550-850
Blue	$110-250	Marigold	$295-505
Marigold	$90-160		

Cherry Blossoms

Water set		Tumbler	
Cobalt blue	$260-360	Cobalt blue	$22-32
Water pitcher			
Cobalt blue	$130-160		

Coin Dot
by Fenton

Bowl, 7-9.25"	
Amethyst	$30-55
Green	$50-65
Marigold	$20-35

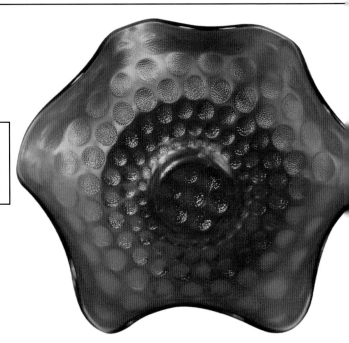

Coin Spot by Dugan and Diamond

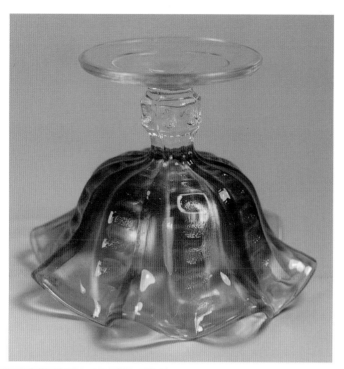

Another view of marigold Coin Spot compote.

Compote		Peach opalescent	$70-180
Cobalt	$525-650	Purple	$75-120
Marigold	$30-45		

Crackle Glass by Imperial

Candlesticks, pair		Water set (with four glasses)	
Marigold	$22-38	Marigold	$70-150
Tumbler			
Marigold	$8-12		

Daisy and Little Flowers by Northwood

Water set	
Cobalt blue	$350-450
Tumbler	
Cobalt blue	$50-65

Diamond and File by Fenton

Exterior of marigold Diamond and File bowl, 7.5", $35-45.

Bowl, 7-9"	
Marigold	$50-60

Diamond Point Columns by Fenton

Vase, 5-6"	
Amethyst	$25-45
Green	$35-60
Marigold	$42-65
Vase, 7-12"	
Amethyst	$32-48
Green	$38-70

Marigold Diamond Point Columns vase,
5.75".

Double Stem Rose by Dugan

Alternate view of Double Stem Rose ruffled marigold bowl.

Interior of Double Stem Rose ruffled marigold bowl.

Bowl, ice cream shape, candy ribbon edge, or ruffled, around 8".		Plate	
Amethyst	$75-170	Amethyst	$320-400
Blue	$150-225	Marigold	$45-55
Marigold	$40-55	Peach Opalescent	$180-225
Peach Opalescent	$55-75	White	$125-195
White	$120-175		

Dragon and Lotus by Fenton

Bowl, ice cream, ruffled, or ribbon edge.
Amber	$125-225
Amethyst	$125-215
Aqua opalescent	$1900-2200
Blue	$150-210
Green	$155-215
Marigold	$65-95
Peach opalescent (ruffled)	$450-750
Red	$2800-4200
Smoke (ruffled)	$195-325

Feathered Arrow
A rare pattern, possibly by Millersburg.

Exterior of marigold Feathered Arrow bowl. $670-690.

Fine Cut & Roses by Northwood

Exterior of Fine Cut and Roses
rosebowl.

Rosebowl with plain interior		Candy dish with plain interior	
Amethyst	$95-150	Amethyst	$40-95
Green	$190-325	Green	$75-150
Marigold	$110-185	Marigold	$35-75
Rosebowl with elaborate interior		Candy dish with elaborate interior	
Amethyst	$140-325	Amethyst	$65-90
Ice Blue	$245-395	Ice blue	$200-350
Marigold	$70-110	Ice green	$210-300
White	$275-410		

Fine Rib by Northwood

Amethyst/purple	$45-75
Green	$40-55
Marigold	$30-40
Sapphire	$200-250

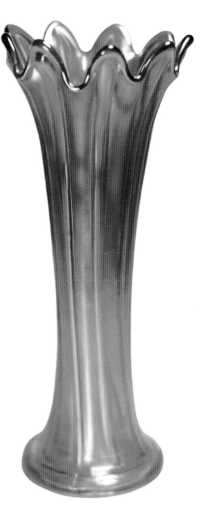

Fruits and Flowers by Northwood

Exterior of Fruits and Flowers bowl to show basketweave pattern, 9".

Bowl, around 7"		Plate, 7-7.5"	
Amethyst/purple	$55-95	Amethyst/purple	$120-200
Blue	$135-205	Green	$225-325
Green	$60-98	Marigold	$110-195
Marigold	$40-45		
		Plate, 8-9"	
Bowl, 9-10"		Marigold	$135-215
Amethyst/purple	$95-145		
Green	$100-165		
Marigold	$55-80		
Violet	$290-325		

Opposite page:

Bowl, 5"	
Peach Opalescent	$65-95
Bowl, 8.5-10.5"	
Marigold	$55-65
Peach Opalescent	$130-250

42

Garden Path by Dugan

Exterior of marigold Garden Path bowl with Soda Gold exterior pattern, 8.5".

Grape and Cable by Fenton

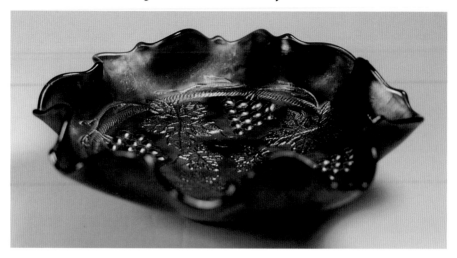

Interior of bowl to show Fenton's Grape and Cable pattern.

Bowl, 7-8"		Plate, 9"	
Blue	$60-80	Blue	$225-275
Green	$70-90	Green	$175-195
Marigold	$55-65	Marigold	$125-175
Red	$700-1000		

Grape and Cable by Northwood

Berry bowl, 5-6"		Marigold	$35-65
Amethyst	$20-45		
Green	$35-60	Bowl, pie crust edge, 8-9"	
Marigold	$25-35	Amethyst	$65-110
		Emerald green	$175-225
Bowl, 7-7.5"		Green	$60-100
Amethyst	$68-98	Marigold	$55-100
Green	$35-55		

White Northwood Grape and Cable bowl, 11".

Bottom left:

Large berry bowl, 10-11"
Amethyst $110-175
Marigold $65-110

Berry set, made up of seven pieces
Green $220-320
Marigold $165-265

Bowl, small ice cream shape
Blue $95-175
White $75-125

Bowl, large ice cream, 10-11"
Amethyst $245-345
Green $375-500
Marigold $145-235
White $235-360

Breakfast set (sugar and creamer)
Amethyst $150-235
Green $155-260
Marigold $125-175

Cup and saucer
Amethyst $175-300
Marigold $190-375
White $145-235

Cologne bottle with stopper
Amethyst $225-295
Marigold $125-185
Purple $300-395

Northwood Grape and Cable hatpin holder.

Hatpin holder
Amethyst $265-395
Emerald green $765-990
Green $285-395
Lavender $590-660
Marigold $245-360
White $1700-1900

47

Amethyst Northwood Grape and Cable
powder jar without lid. $15-25.

Powder Jar			Fernery		
Amethyst/purple	$175-195		Marigold	$550-950
Lavender	$275-375		Purple	$700-1100
Marigold	$95-125		White	$660-820
Powder jar (without lid)			Butter dish		
Amethyst/purple	$15-25		Amethyst	$150-230
Lavender	$35-55		Green	$190-260
Marigold	$15-25		Marigold	$95-165
Humidor			Creamer		
Amethyst	$320-350		Amethyst	$70-125
Blue	$490-535		Marigold	$50-70
Marigold	$280-465			
			Spooner		
Humidor, stippled			Amethyst	$95-150
Blue	$695		Marigold	$65-100
Marigold	$425-525			

Left. Northwood Grape and Cable covered butter dish.
Right. Northwood Grape and Cable stopper to cologne.

Sugar, covered		Water pitcher, table size	
Amethyst	$110-175	Amethyst	$225-300
Marigold	$68-98	Green	$260-410
		Marigold	$250-350
		Smoke	$495-750

Tumbler for regular water set	
Amethyst	$35-60
Green	$40-75
Marigold	$35-50
Plate, 7-8"	
Amethyst	$150-225
Amber	$90-110
Marigold	$200-275
Plate, 8.5-9"	
Amethyst	$175-250
Marigold	$110-195

Northwood Grape and Cable water tumbler.

Grape and Cable Variant by Northwood

Bowl		Plate	
Amethyst	$110-200	Amethyst	$175-250
Blue	$310-450	Clambroth	$295-350
Marigold	$55-85	Marigold	$175-275
		Marigold (stippled)	$250-400
		Sapphire Blue (stippled)	$3400-3750

Grape Delight by Dugan

Rosebowl		Nut bowl (pictured)	
Amethyst	$55-95	Amethyst	$75-120
Blue	$55-85	Blue	$65-150
Marigold	$50-85	Purple	$295-500
White	$55-95		

Hobstar by Imperial

Bowls, 5-7"		Purple	$80-120
Marigold	$22-28		
Purple	$50-65	Punch bowl and base	
		Emerald	$595-650
Table set		Marigold	$275-300
Marigold	$175-225		
		Punch cup	
Bowl, 8-10"		Emerald	$60-75
Marigold	$30-35	Marigold	$35-45

Hobstar and Arches by Imperial

Interior view of
Hobstar & Arches
marigold bowl, 8.5".

Exterior of
Hobstar & Arches
marigold bowl.

Bowl, 8.5-9.5"	
Helios	$65-80
Marigold	$35-45
Purple	$110-135

Holly by Fenton

Left. Interior of Holly marigold compote.
Right. Interior of Holly cobalt blue compote.

Bowl, ruffled or candy ribbon edge, 9"			
Amethyst	$110-125	White	$110-160
Blue	$75-85		
Green	$150-200	Bowl, ice cream or round	
Marigold	$55-75	Blue	$90-130
Red	$1300-1900	Marigold	$40-60

Bowl, ruffled or candy ribbon edge, 9" — Vaseline $125-175

Blue ruffled Holly
bowl, 9".

Another view of blue ruffled Holly bowl.

Plate, 9-10"		Compote	
Amethyst	$650-875	Blue	$55-95
Blue	$250-450	Green	$150-225
Clambroth	$175-250	Marigold	$40-65
Green	$900-1,500	Pink	$70-100
Marigold	$225-300	Red	$900-1600
White	$200-300		

Holly & Berry by Dugan

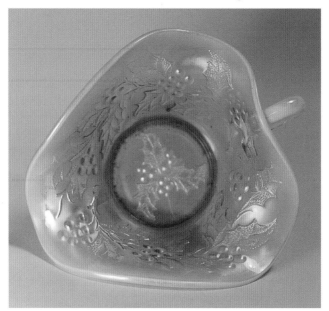

Alternate view of Holly & Berry peach opalescent nappy.

Bowl, ruffled, 7-8"
    Amethyst $90-160
    Peach opalescent $55-85

Nappy, ruffled or three cornered
    Amethyst $65-95
    Peach opalescent $55-75

Imperial Grape

Imperial Grape marigold berry bowl, 5.5".

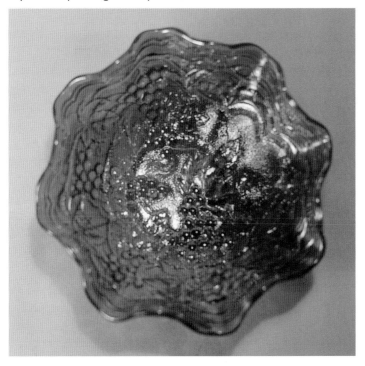

Exterior of Imperial Grape marigold bowl.

Berry bowl, 5-6"		Bowl, 8-9"	
Amber	$35-45	Amber	$40-65
Marigold	$20-30	Clambroth (ruffled)	$35-55
Purple	$20-30	Helios	$20-30
		Lavender (ruffled)	$90-110
Bowl, 7"		Marigold	$25-40
Marigold	$20-30	Purple	$60-95
Purple	$40-55		

Imperial Grape marigold bowl, 9".

Exterior of Imperial Grape marigold bowl.

Bowl, 10-11"		Marigold	$65-125
Blue	$245-260	Purple	$1800-3000
Marigold	$35-60		
Purple	$95-175	Compote	
Smoke	$60-95	Amber	$35-55
		Helios	$50-75
Plate, 6"		Marigold	$30-60
Helios	$60-95	Purple	$60-90
Marigold	$50-85	Smoke	$60-90
Purple	$160-250		
		Cup and Saucer	
Plate, 9"		Clambroth	$30-40
Amber	$700-1000	Helios	$35-60
Clambroth	$55-90	Marigold	$55-75

Imperial Grape purple decanter without stopper. $60-70.

Imperial Grape marigold decanter with stopper, 12.5".

Decanter with stopper	
Marigold	$95-125
Purple	$175-195

Water set, seven pieces	
Marigold	$155-225
Purple	$450-650
Smoke	$500-650
Pitcher, water	
Marigold	$60-110
Purple	$350-375
Tumbler	
Marigold	$25-30
Purple	$50-55
Smoke	$55-65

Imperial Rose, also known as Open Rose

Imperial Rose marigold plate, 9".

Imperial Rose Prices

Bowl, small berry		Marigold	$25-40
Blue	$60-80	Purple	$120-150
Marigold	$15-20		
Smoke	$25-35	Plate, 9"	
		Amber	$210-325
Bowl, 7-9"		Green	$95-165
Amber	$25-45	Marigold	$95-120
Cobalt blue	$110-300	Purple	$1475-2200

Leaf Rays by Dugan

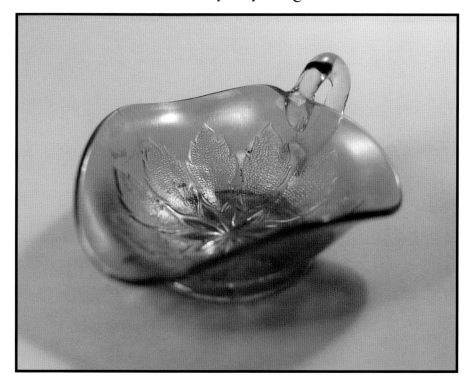

Nappy (spade shape)		Marigold	$20-35
Amethyst/purple	$45-75	Peach opalescent	$30-45
Lavender	$50-65		

Little Flowers by Fenton

Bowl, ice cream shape, ruffled, or candy ribbon edge, 9.5".		Bowl, small berry, 5-6"	
Amethyst	$80-150	Amethyst	$75-150
Blue	$95-160	Blue	$55-85
Marigold	$75-95	Marigold	$25-40
		Plate, 6-7"	
		Blue	$215-250
		Marigold	$225-275

Loganberry by Imperial

Left:

Vase	
Amber	$750-1000
Emerald	$550-1000
Helios	$300-400
Marigold	$275-350
Purple	$700-1300

Louisa by Westmoreland

Amethyst Louisa footed bowl, 9".

Bowl	
Amethyst	$40-50
Green	$50-60
Rosebowl, footed	
Amethyst	$45-55
Green	$55-65
Marigold	$45-55

Lustre and Clear by Imperial

Breakfast set (made up of creamer and sugar)		Plate	
		Clambroth	$20-25
Marigold	$50-60	Marigold	$35-40

Lustre Flute by Northwood

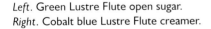

Left. Green Lustre Flute open sugar.
Right. Cobalt blue Lustre Flute creamer.

Marigold Lustre Flute tumbler whimsey. $50-60.

Breakfast set (made up of creamer and sugar)	
Green	$80-110
Cobalt blue	$45-55

Nesting Swan by Millersburg

Bowl, 10"		Green, square	$850-1200
Amethyst, ruffled	$335-450	Marigold, ruffled	$200-275
Blue	$2500-2800	Marigold (ruffled with	
Green, ruffled	$300-500	blue iridescence)	$275-375

Nippon by Northwood

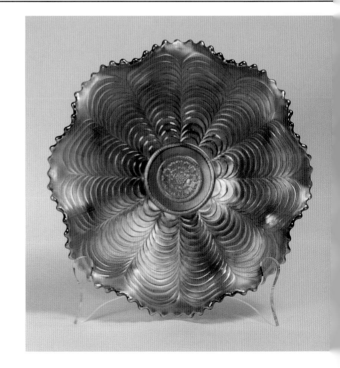

Basketweave exterior of green Nippon bowl.

Bowl, ruffled	
Green	$275-375
Ice blue	$325-425
Marigold	$125-225

Octagon by Imperial

Pitcher, water	
Marigold (large)	$175-250
Marigold (small)	$125-200
Purple (large)	$600-700
Tumbler	
Marigold	$25-45
Purple	$90-125
Vase, 8"	
Marigold	$75-125

71

Open Edge by Fenton

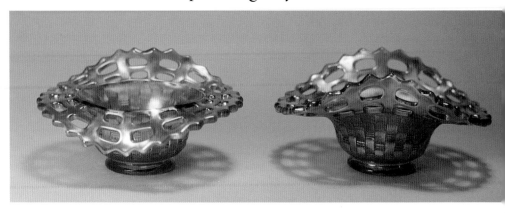

Basket/hat, small, basketweave, ruffled
- Aqua $75-150
- Marigold $30-40
- Red $225-375

Basket/hat, small, basketweave, two sides up
- Cobalt blue $50-80
- Green $250-350
- Marigold $25-35
- Red $350-475
- White $275-295

Basket/hat, small, basketweave, Jack-in-the-Pulpit shape
- Amethyst $175-275
- Blue $65-175
- Marigold $45-55

Basket/hat, basketweave, 5-7"
- Ice blue (ice cream shape) $225-350
- Ice blue (with two sides up) $225-350
- Marigold $45-75
- Red $350-550
- White $150-195

Orange Tree by Fenton

Orange Tree by Fenton Prices

Plate, 9"		Blue	$95-225
Blue	$575-1200	Marigold	$80-165
Clambroth	$200-275		
Marigold	$325-350	Compote	
White	$175-350	Blue	$55-95
		Marigold (ruffled)	$45-55
Bowl, collar base, 8-9"			
Blue	$95-125	Hatpin Holder (shown)	
Clambroth	$45-125	Blue	$225-295
Marigold	$60-95	Marigold	$225-395
Red	$2500-3500	White	$695-825
Sapphire	$250-295		
White	$95-175	Powder Jar (shown)	
		Blue	$95-175
Bowl, fruit or orange with scroll feet,		Green	$450-650
10" (shown)		Marigold	$75-175
Blue	$175-250		
Marigold	$90-150	Tumbler	
		Blue	$55-85
Breakfast set (made up of creamer and		Marigold	$50-75
sugar)		White	$65-95
Amethyst	$90-175		

Peacock and Grape by Fenton

Bowl, ice cream shape, ruffled shape,
   or candy ribbon edge, 8-9"
   Amber, ice cream
   shape $495-595
   Blue $150-250
   Amethyst/black $125-195
   Marigold $65-85
   Red $980-1550

Nut bowl, deep, ice cream
   shape, ruffled
   Blue $95-175
   Marigold $50-70

Peacock and Urn by Fenton

Bowl, ice cream shape or ruffled edge, 8-9"	
Amethyst	$250-350
Blue	$175-275
Marigold	$95-175
White	$150-225
Plate, 9"	
Blue	$525-725
Marigold	$350-450
White	$395-495
Compote (shown)	
Aqua	$125-195
Blue	$95-125
Marigold	$35-65
Red	$600-800
Vaseline	$145-195
White	$175-250

Peacock and Urn by Northwood

Ice cream set, made up of seven pieces	
White	$800-1000

Bowl, large ice cream, not stippled, 9"	
Amethyst/purple	$500-695
Clambroth	$725-795
Green	$2000-5000
Ice blue	$900-1200
Ice green	$1200-1400
Marigold	$400-600
White	$350-600

Bowl, small ice cream, 5-6" (shown)	
Amethyst/purple	$95-175
Blue	$85-195
Ice blue	$250-375
Marigold	$95-375
White	$125-225

Peacock at the Fountain by Northwood

Bowl, small berry		
Amethyst/purple	$45-65	
Blue	$35-85	
Green	$65-125	
Marigold	$25-55	
Water set, seven piece		
Amethyst/purple	$425-595	
Blue	$525-725	
Marigold	$325-395	
Pitcher, water		
Amethyst/purple	$425-595	
Blue	$550-725	
Marigold	$350-395	
Tumbler		
Amethyst/purple	$55-65	
Blue	$65-85	
Ice blue	$165-265	
Marigold	$40-50	
White	$175-275	

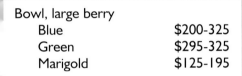

Bowl, large berry	
Blue	$200-325
Green	$295-325
Marigold	$125-195

Peacock Tail by Fenton

Bowl, candy ribbon edge, round, or
   ruffled, 7"
     Amethyst $35-55
     Green $25-65
     Marigold $50-85

Bonbon, stemmed with two
   handles
     Amethyst $45-85
     Blue $55-75
     Green $45-95
     Marigold $30-70

Compote, ruffled
     Amethyst $30-50
     Blue $35-55
     Green $50-70
     Marigold $30-40

Puzzle by Dugan

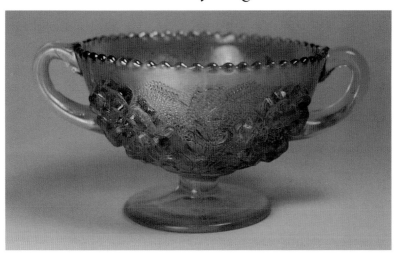

Compote, also called bonbon		Marigold	$35-45
Amethyst/purple	$65-75	Peach opalescent	$80-125
Blue	$100-145	White	$80-125

Question Marks by Dugan

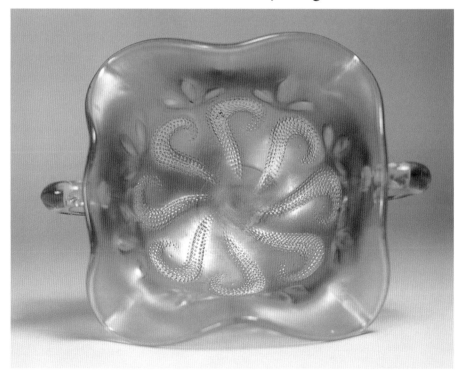

Bonbon		Compote	
Amethyst/purple	$35-65	Amethyst	$55-75
Marigold	$35-45	Marigold	$40-50
Peach opalescent	$45-65	Peach opalescent	
White	$35-50	(crimped)	$75-85
		White	$80-90

Ribbon Tie by Fenton

Bowl, 8-9"	
Amethyst	$95-225
Blue	$130-180
Marigold	$65-125

Plate, also called low ruffle bowl, 9-10"	
Amethyst	$85-125
Blue	$195-295

Another view of blue Ribbon Tie bowl, 8.5".

Ripple Vase by Imperial

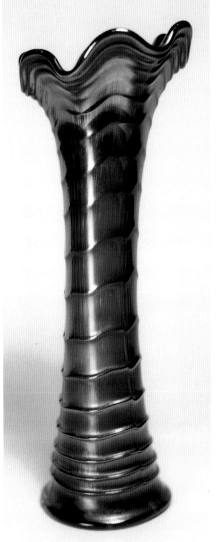

Small, 4-7"	
Helios	$75-245
Marigold	$35-125
Purple	$95-125

Standard, 7-12"	
Blue	$225-275
Blue violet	$175-575
Helios	$35-125
Marigold	$35-75
Purple	$85-130
White	$145-225

Midsize, 12-15"	
Amber	$195-225
Marigold	$55-85
Teal	$60-70

Funeral size, 15-21"	
Marigold	$150-295
Purple	$350-450

Amethyst Ripple vase, 11.5".

Rosette by Northwood

Exterior of amethyst Rosette bowl, 9".

Bowl, footed, 7-9"	
Amethyst (shown)	$125-145
Marigold	$55-75

Sailboats by Fenton

Bowl, small, 6"	
Aqua (ruffled)	$75-125
Blue	$55-75
Green	$85-125
Marigold	$25-35
Plate, 6"-6.5"	
Blue	$600-900
Marigold	$495-775

Exterior of green Sailboats berry bowl with
Orange Tree exterior pattern, 6".

Scroll Embossed by Imperial

Helios Scroll Embossed plate, 9".

Plate, 9-9.5" (shown)		Marigold	$35-55
Helios green	$75-155	Purple	$75-125
Marigold	$95-225		
Purple	$325-425	Bowl, small	
		Marigold	$25-45
Bowl, 7-9" (shown)		Purple	$55-65
Helios	$15-25		

Shell and Jewel by Westmoreland

Sugar and creamer set	
Green	$55-65
Marigold	$35-65

Ski Star by Dugan

Bowl, berry, 5-6" (shown)		Peach opalescent	$55-95
Peach opalescent	$35-50	Purple	$275-375
Purple	$95-125		
		Plate or bowl with handle	
Bowl, 10-11", crimped or ruffled		Peach opalescent	$125-155

Smooth Rays, made by many companies

Smooth Rays marigold bowl by Imperial, 8". $35-60.

Smooth Rays marigold bowl by Westmoreland, 6". $55-75.

Split Diamond

Butter dish	
Marigold	$45-65
Compote	
Marigold	$35-45
Bowl, 5"	
Marigold (flat dish)	$25-35

Bowl, ice cream shape or ruffled, 7.5"	
Amethyst	$150-250
Blue	$125-225
Green	$125-225
Lavender	
(ice cream shape)	$250-350
Marigold	$85-150
Bowl, ruffled, 10"	
Amethyst	$22-400
Blue	$195-350
Marigold	$110-200
Bowl, ice cream shape, 10-11"	
Blue	$325-475
Marigold	$95-160

Left. Split Diamond marigold butter dish.
Center. Split Diamond compote.
Right. Split Diamond bowl.

Stag and Holly by Fenton

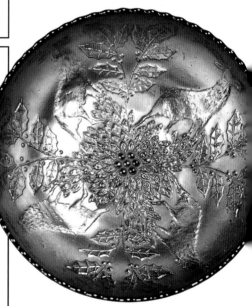

Amethyst Stag and Holly bowl, 7.5".

Star and File by Imperial

Bowl, 8" (shown)		Tumbler (juice)	
Marigold	$25-35	Marigold	$30-50
Nut bowl		Tumbler (iced tea)	
Marigold	$15-35	Marigold	$35-55
Compote			
Marigold	$45-55		

Stippled Rays by Fenton

Exterior of Stippled Rays by Fenton marigold plate and bowls showcasing Scale pattern exterior.

Bowl, 5-10"		Plate, 7"	
Blue	$45-55	Amethyst	$125-150
Green	$30-50	Marigold	$40-80
Marigold	$15-30	Red	$525-1225
Red	$395-450		
Compote		Creamer and sugar set	
Blue	$35-45	Green	$80-125
Green	$50-60	Marigold	$50-75
Marigold	$35-45		

Stippled Rays by Northwood

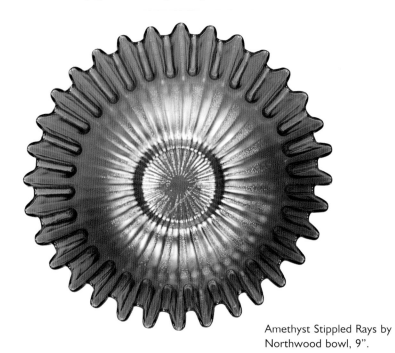

Amethyst Stippled Rays by
Northwood bowl, 9".

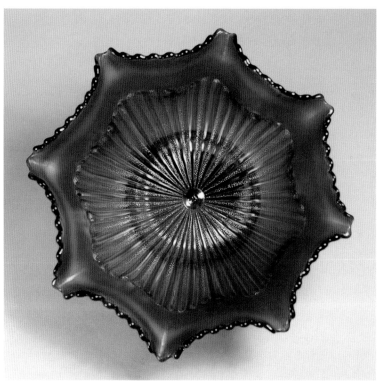

Bowl, pie crust edge		Bowl, ruffled	
Amethyst/purple	$50-60	Amethyst	$35-45
Lavender	$55-65	Green	$75-125
Marigold	$40-50	Marigold	$25-35
		Purple	$45-65

Strawberry by Northwood

Exterior of Amethyst bowl to show exterior basketweave pattern.

Bowl, ruffled, around 9"		Green	$95-175
Amethyst/purple	$155-325	Marigold	$75-125
Green	$175-325	Smoke	$795-925
Marigold	$125-225		
Smoke	$775-875	Plate, with ribbed exterior or plain exterior, around 9"	
Bowl, pie crust edge, around 9" (pictured)		Amethyst/purple	$375-450
		Green	$400-600
Amethyst/purple	$175-225	Marigold	$275-575

Stretch Glass

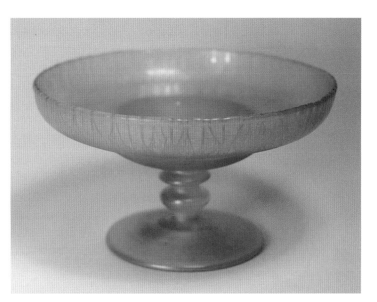

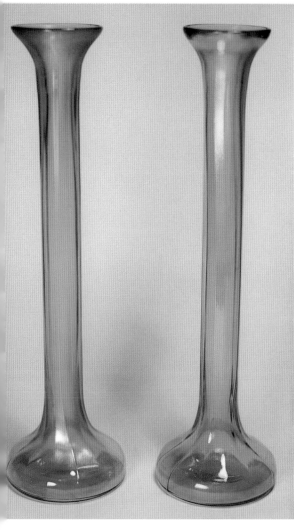

Console set (made up of
   bowl and two candle
   sticks)
   Celeste $30-50
   Olive $225-250
   Red $275-295

Bowl, 7-10"
   Blue opaque $45-55
   Red $50-80

Swirl by Imperial

Vase, 8"	
Smoke	$15-25
Marigold	$20-40

Three Fruits by Northwood

Bowl, plain, 9"		Green	$650-800
Amethyst/purple	$75-160	Marigold	$75-155
Green	$95-185		
Marigold	$75-125	Bowl, pie crust edge, 9"	
Smoke	$395-425	Amethyst/purple	$125-160
		Green	$125-180
Bowl, stippled, 9"		Marigold	$75-125
Amethyst/purple	$150-250	Smoke	$425-525

Three-in-One by Imperials

Bowl	
Marigold	$20-30
Smoke	$35-45
Plate, 6-7"	
Marigold	$45-75
Rosebowl	
Marigold	$95-200

Twins by Imperial

Marigold Twins base for fruit bowl.

Marigold Twins fruit bowl.

Fruit bowl (with base)	
Marigold	$55-95
Pedestal	
Marigold	$10-30

Vintage by Fenton

Small bowl		Marigold	$45-65
Amethyst	$15-35	Red	$2000-3000
Blue	$35-45		
Marigold	$25-55	Plate, 7-8"	
		Amethyst	$450-550
Bowl, 7-8"		Blue	$300-400
Amethyst	$25-45	Green	$325-425
Blue	$50-60	Marigold	$225-325
Green	$35-45		
Marigold	$30-40	Compote	
		Amethyst	$35-55
Bowl, candy ribbon edge or ruffled, 9"		Blue	$60-80
Amethyst	$60-70	Green	$75-95
Blue	$75-125	Marigold	$35-45
Green	$60-90		

Imperial's Vintage

Imperial's Vintage server with center handle, the only shape known in this pattern, 10.5".

Clambroth	$30-40
Marigold	$35-45
Smoke	$40-50

Windflower by Dugan

Bowl, 8-9"		Nappy	
Amethyst/purple	$70-100	Amethyst/purple	$85-125
Blue	$75-125	Marigold	$35-85
Marigold	$25-45		
Plate, 8-9"			
Marigold	$125-175		

Wishbone and Spades by Dugan

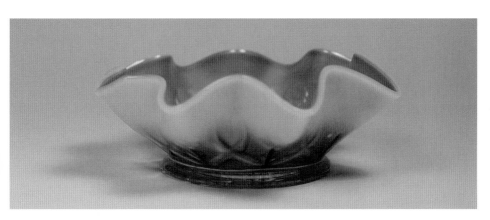

Plate, 6-7"		Bowl, ice cream shape or ruffled, 9-10"	
Peach opalescent	$250-350	Peach opalescent	
Purple	$500-900	(ruffled)	$225-325
		Peach opalescent	
		(ice cream shape)	$275-325

Chapter Three
Contemporary Carnival Glass

Fenton 75th Anniversary plate. $45-55.

Left. "Sixth Day of Christmas" commemorative plate, 1976. $45-55.
Right. "Sixth Day of Christmas" plate, 1975. $45-55.

Bicentennial square toothpick holder by Joe St. Clair. $25-45.

Another view of Bicentennial toothpick holder.

Another view of Bicentennial toothpick holder depicting Liberty Bell.

Smoke colored Daisy Basket by Imperial. $15-25.

Imperial 474 pink salt and pepper shakers. $15-25.

Imperial 474 compote. $20-30.

Another view of compote.

Interior view of compote.

Jeannette covered dish in the shape of a duck. $35-45.

Eastern Star compote by Imperial. $35-45.

Harvest by Indiana serving tray. $15-25.
Harvest creamer and sugar. $35-45.

Four tumblers from Harvest pattern by Indiana. $15-20 each.

Footed pitcher from Harvest pattern by Indiana. $25-35.

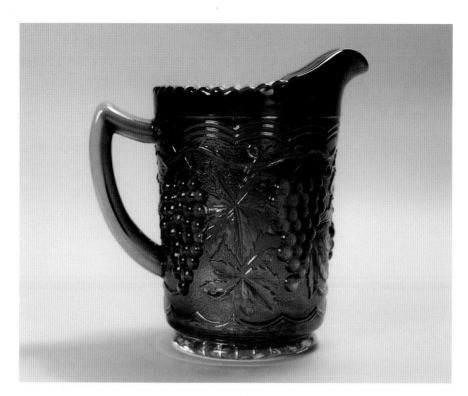

Small pitcher from Harvest pattern by Indiana. $35-45.

Humidor from Harvest
pattern by Indiana.
$45-65.

Set of four 9-oz. goblets in Harvest pattern by Indiana. $15-20. each.

Geometric bowl, ("Hattie") by Imperial. $15-20.

Another view of bowl's exterior.

Hobnail vase by Fenton. $30-45.

Lustre Rose marigold table set. $55-75.

Left. Lustre Rose by Imperial, green butter dish with cover. $25-35.
Center. Lustre Rose by Imperial, smoke butter dish with cover. $25-35.
Right. Lustre Rose by Imperial, marigold butter dish with cover. $25-35.

Cobalt blue pitcher and four tumblers, in Lustre Rose by Imperial. $175-195.

Cobalt blue fernery, in Lustre Rose by Imperial . $45-55.

Another view of Lustre Rose cobalt blue fernery.

Planter/vase in Mermaid by Fenton. $45-55.

Left. Marigold compote, Octagon by Imperial. $15-25.
Right. Smoke compote, Octagon by Imperial. $15-25.

Octagon Optic
tumbler. $20-25.

Three Octagon Optic toothpick
holders. $5-10 each.

White nappy in Pansy by Imperial. $10-15.

Another view of nappy in Pansy by Imperial to show Diamond Quilted pattern on exterior.

Pitcher by Fenton. $125-135.

Ice blue water set in Robin by Imperial/Lenox. $55-75.

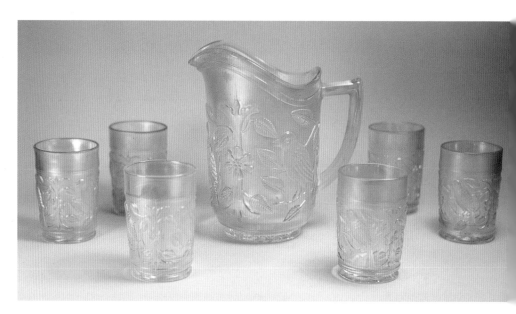

White water set in Robin by Imperial/Lenox. $55-75.

Sugar dish, Strutting Peacock by Westmoreland. $65-75.

Pink water set, Tiger Lily by Imperial/Lenox. $75-95.

Ice blue water set, Tiger Lily by Imperial/Lenox. $75-95.

Left. Toothpick holder with cherry motif by Summit. $5-8.
Right. Indianhead toothpick holder by Joe St. Clair. $5-8.

8-oz. goblet, Tulip and Cane by Imperial, 6.5". $10-15.

Bowl, Windmill by Imperial, 8". $35-45.

Water set, Windmill by Imperial. $175-225.

Bibliography

Burns, Carl O. *Imperial Carnival Glass*. Paducah, Kentucky: Collector Books, 1996.

Cosentino, Geraldine, and Regina Stewart. *Carnival Glass: A Guide for the Beginning Collector*. New York: Golden Press, 1976.

Doty, David. *A Field Guide to Carnival Glass*. Marietta, Ohio: Glass Press, Inc., 1998.

Edwards, Bill. *Imperial Carnival Glass: The Early Years*. Paducah, Kentucky: Collector Books, 1980.

Edwards, Bill. *Millersburg: The Queen of Carnival Glass*. Paducah, Kentucky: Collector Books, 1979.

Edwards, Bill, and Mike Carwile. *Standard Encyclopedia of Carnival Glass*. Paducah, Kentucky: Collector Books, 1998.

George, Karen. *Contemporary Carnival Glass Reference Book*. Corydon, Iowa: Karen George, 2000.

Heacock, William. *Fenton Glass: The Third Twenty-Five Years 1956-1980*. Marietta, Ohio: O-Val Advertising Corp., 1989.

Heacock, William, and James Measell and Barry Wiggins. *Harry Northwood: The Early Years 1881-1900*. Marietta, Ohio: Antique Publications, 1990.

Heacock, William, and James Measell and Barry Wiggins. *Harry Northwood: The Wheeling Years 1901-1925*. Marietta, Ohio: Antique Publications, 1990.

Quintin-Baxendale, Marion. *Collecting Carnival Glass*. London: Francis Joseph Publications, 1988.

Thistlewood, Glen and Stephen. *Carnival Glass: The Magic and the Mystery*. Atglen, Pennsylvania: Schiffer Publishing Ltd., 1998.

Weatherman, Hazel Marie. *Colored Glassware of the Depression Era 2*. Ozark, Missouri: Weatherman Glassbooks, 1974.